Lóide Jacob

Social Entrepreneurship

Lóide Jacob

Social Entrepreneurship

Social problem solving

ScienciaScripts

Imprint

Any brand names and product names mentioned in this book are subject to trademark, brand or patent protection and are trademarks or registered trademarks of their respective holders. The use of brand names, product names, common names, trade names, product descriptions etc. even without a particular marking in this work is in no way to be construed to mean that such names may be regarded as unrestricted in respect of trademark and brand protection legislation and could thus be used by anyone.

Cover image: www.ingimage.com

This book is a translation from the original published under ISBN 978-620-2-56264-5.

Publisher:
Sciencia Scripts
is a trademark of
International Book Market Service Ltd., member of OmniScriptum Publishing Group
17 Meldrum Street, Beau Bassin 71504, Mauritius
Printed at: see last page
ISBN: 978-620-2-76917-4

Copyright © Lóide Jacob
Copyright © 2021 International Book Market Service Ltd., member of OmniScriptum Publishing Group

CONTENTS

INTRODUCTION

The social entrepreneur must be able to identify a social problem, combine resources and take risks to solve it, raise funding, establish partnerships and create social value with the solution of the problem identified. These are skills that this book proposes to develop in its audience. This book presents the concepts of social entrepreneurship in a clear and practical way, to benefit not only students but also organizations that develop social projects. The social entrepreneur is someone who is convinced that poverty or disability is an external or system or society imposition. In other words, no one chooses to be born poor. And because it is an imposition it can be removed. Today, Social Entrepreneurship is applied in various sectors of social life, and is very relevant to activities involving communities on the Internet. Social Entrepreneurship is an area of knowledge that belongs to the social sciences and seeks to reconcile two fundamental ideas (a) the creation of social value and (b) the creation of economic value. But it is to retain that, the end of Social Entrepreneurship is the maximization of social impact understood as the lasting change that occurs in the lives of the beneficiaries of a social entrepreneurship initiative. The term social entrepreneur was coined by Bill Drayton in the 1980s. Drayton is responsible for creating Ashoka, a global, non-profit organization that pioneered the work and support of social entrepreneurs. Ashoka had its first focus in India and is now present in over 60 countries. (Oliveira, 2004).

The structure of this bookfollows thelogic ofdeveloping a social idea. Inchapter 1, the mainconcepts that define social entrepreneurship arepresented,the objective is to describe the thought of social entrepreneurship. In chapter 2, the main concepts of innovation are presented, their theories andpractices, the objective is to describe innovation thinking. Inchapter 3,thedevelopment model of social entrepreneurship is presented, describing its stages, the objective to describe the mechanism of functioning of social entrepreneurship. Inchapter 4,the main concepts of impact assessment are presented, starting by clarifying the definition of indicators, the objective is to describe social impact assessment thinking. Inchapter 5, theoretical social entrepreneurship financing instruments arepresented andexisting instruments in the Angolan market, the objective is to describe social financing thinking. And finally, inchapter 6, the main concepts of social marketing are presented, with the stages of developing a marketing plan for a social enterprise, the objective is to describe social marketing thinking. All theory and thinking is developed, taking into account social practice through examples and graphic representations.

CHAPTER 1

CONCEPT OF SOCIAL ENTREPRENEURSHIP

The genesis of the term "entrepreneurship" is much discussed and there is stillno real consensus. However, mostreferences converge that the term " *entrepreneur* " is derived from the French word *entrepreneur*, which means the individual who takes risks by starting something new, as was initially referred to in1725 by Richard Cantilon (Dees, 2001; Filion 1999). Around the 19th century, the concept of entrepreneurship took on a new outline with the contributions presented by Jean Baptiste Say ,associating the concept with the creation of new ventures/businesses and the entrepreneur as the one responsible for bringing together the factors of production, establishing the value of wages, interest paid, rent and profits that belong to him (Dees,2001; Filion 1999). Based on Cantilon and Say, Schumpeter improves the concept of entrepreneurship by associating the term with "creativity", Schumpeter (1947), defended the importance of innovation in the entrepreneurship process as well as the role of entrepreneurship in economic development. With the evolution ofcompetitive strategiesfocused on the abuse of natural resources, the increase in social inequalities and the accumulation of wealth, a new movement of social responsibility began, which led entrepreneurshipto evolve into social entrepreneurship.

1.1. DEFINITION OF SOCIAL ENTREPRENEURSHIP

The term social entrepreneur was coined by Bill Drayton in the 1980s, Drayton is responsible for creating Ashoka, a worldwide non-profit organisationthat pioneered the work and support of social entrepreneurs. Ashoka had its first focus in India and today

is present in over 60 countries (Oliveira, 2004).

From Drayton to the present day, the term "Social Entrepreneurship" has had much application, from people and organisations and the support of organisations promoting it, such as

- ✓ Ashoka: worldwide network for information exchange, collaboration and dissemination of projects;
- ✓ Kiva: investment in micro and small entrepreneurs from all over the world;
- ✓ Artemísia: creation and development of business models related to social entrepreneurship.

This evolution of application ofthe then new termbuilds aseries of definitions as much as the diversityof itsapplications, in ways that do not exist today, a consensual definition, butseveral definitions according to the nature of their applications. The Institute of Social Entrepreneurship defines social entrepreneurship as "an innovative approach aimed at better solving social problems, with a clear social mission, sustainable, replicable in other contexts, and capable of producing social impact on a large scale. For Alvord, Brown and Letts (2004) Social entrepreneurship "creates innovative solutions to immediate social problems and mobilises the ideas, capabilities, resources, and social arrangementsneeded for sustainable social transformation". Peredo and McLean (2006) consider that social entrepreneurship is exercised when a person or a group: (a) aims to create social value;(b) demonstrates an ability to recognise and take advantage of opportunities that create value; (c) employs innovation;(d) is willing to accept an above-average level of risk to create and disseminate social value creation; and (e) is particularly resourceful and not intimidated by the scarcity of resources in pursuing its social initiative.For Dees (2001) social entrepreneurs assume the role of agents of change in the social sector by: (a) adopting a mission to create social value in a sustainable manner;(b) recognizing and capturing new opportunities that serve their mission;(c) committing to a process of continuous innovation, adaptation and learning;(e) acting boldly without being limited to the resources held at any given time;(f) demonstrating a high level of accountability for the elements served and the results generated .According to Santos (2009 apud Austin, Stevenson and Wei-Skillern, 2006), social entrepreneurship "is an entrepreneurial activity with a social purpose. And for Nicholls and Huybrechts (2011) social entrepreneurship is the dynamic process by which specific types of individuals deserving the name "social entrepreneurs" create and develop organizations that can be defined as "social enterprises". Social enterprises" are a subset of such activities in which business models are used as the vehicle by which social objects are achieved (Thompson, 2008). Abu-saifan (2012) discusses a delimitation for the definition of social entrepreneurship, and criticizes the fact that individuals even when publicly recognized as social entrepreneurs for their contributions to improving community well-being arenot legitimizedby the academic field. The author proposes that tobecome a mainstream in the literature of entrepreneurship, social entrepreneurship needs to be adequately defined and requires a theoretical framework that links it to the theory of entrepreneurship . According to his theoreticalframework, cited by the authors below, the characteristics of social entrepreneurship are:

a)   Mission and persistentleader (Bomstein, 1998);

b)   Emotionally stable and sociallyvaluable(Thompsonet al.(2000);

c)   Highly responsible, dedicated and socially alert changeagent (Dees, 1998);

d)   Opinionleader (Brinckerhoff, 2009);

e)   Manager and leader (Leadbeater, 1997);

f)   Innovative and innovative (Zahra et al., 2008).

According to Thompson (2008) For a social entrepreneurship initiative to be considered as such it must meet the following requirements:

a)   It has a social purpose;

b)   Its assets and wealth are used to create benefits for the community;

c)   It seeks the benefit of the community with trade activities that can be partly paid for by the same community;

d)   Profits and surpluses are reinvested in business and the community and not distributed to shareholders;

e)   Employees (or members) have some role in decision-making and governance; that is, they follow a *bottom-up*management model ;

f)   The company takes responsibility for its employees and the community;

g)   The initiative must generate either balanced economic, social and environmental returns on a double or triple basis.

A social entrepreneur is someone who solves problems by using his or her ideas and others' ideas and combining them effectively to build solutions that will be implemented. More than an inventor, a social entrepreneur is an architect of solutions to important social problems. A good entrepreneur does not cling to his own ideas and has the humility to see his solution evolving and being transformed. Table 1 below presents some of the skills of the social entrepreneur.

Table 1: Social Entrepreneur Skills

Skills	Knowledge	Skills	Attitudes
Ability to identify a social problem	Definition ofSocial Entrepreneurship	Use of strategic management and quality managementtools	Beingproactive
Ability to combine resources to generate solution	Social BusinessModel ; Innovation and Project Management	Use of social project management and business model creation tools	Taking the lead
Ability to assume calculated risks	Impact chain and project management	Use of feasibility studies and social impact assessment tools	Being dissatisfied
Ability to raise funding to generate solution	Ecosystem of social entrepreneurship and Social Marketing	Doing oral and written communication, doing public relations, using sales techniques, doing group work, making partnerships	Have commitment
Ability to test the pilot project and realize the solution	Implementation structure ofthe social business model	Make social business plan	Having responsibility
Ability to be accountable	Social impact assessment	Reporting	Having honesty
Mentoring skills	Social marketing	Making influences	Have legacy

Source: Own Elaboration

1.2. ECOSYSTEM OF SOCIAL ENTREPRENEURSHIP

The idea of ecosystem of entrepreneurship, derives from the concept of ecosystem services. Ecosystem servicescan be perceived as a contribution of natural capital to human well-being, which is formed by interaction with human, social and built capital. Ecosystems cannot provide benefit to people without the presence of people (human capital), their communities (social capital) and their built environment (built capital), (Kasparinskis, Ruskule, Vinogradovs, Pecina, 2018).

Figure 1: Representation of ecosystem services

Source: own elaboration.

In this way, the ecosystem of social entrepreneurship is formed, when all the necessaryconditions for the transfer of capital to solve a social problemarepresent . The social entrepreneur must understand the dynamicsofthe functioningof his ecosystem.

Figure 2: Ecosystem of Social Entrepreneurship

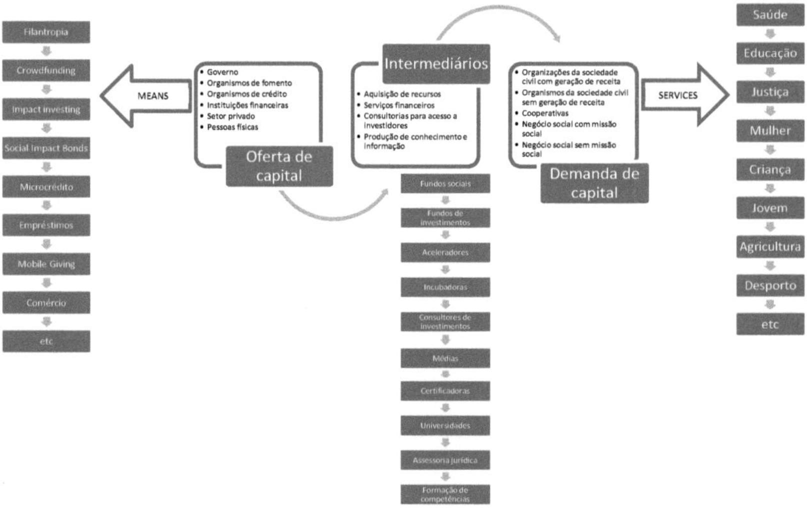

Source: own elaboration

For Isenberg (2011) an entrepreneurial ecosystem is made up of six major constructs:(1) Policies (factors related to government regulations, tax incentives and other strategies to encourage entrepreneurship); (2)Finance (structure to attract small investors, angel investors, large *private equity*funds, among others); (3) Culture (how is the tolerance to error, how valued are successful entrepreneurs, what is the ambition of the population to undertake, among others);(4) Support (how to support infrastructure and professional services to nascent businesses); (5) Human Capital (addresses issues related to vocational training for entrepreneurship and training) and (6) Markets (parameters related to regionalisation of the economy, diversification, among others).

1.3. SOCIALBUSINESS MODEL

The business model is the integrated vision of the process of identifying and using resources, competencies and partnerships to create and deliver value to its customers and shareholders. The business models of social entrepreneurship are social businesses (Elkington & Hartigan, 2017;Yunus, 2010). In general, three models are presented:

✓   Model 1 -Non-profit enterprises financed (Tcherneva, 2012; Salavou and Manolopoulos, 2019):

a)   A public good/service is being delivered to the most economically vulnerable, who have no access to or cannot pay for the service provided;

b)   Both the entrepreneur and the organization are catalysts for change, with the central objective of allowing the direct beneficiaries to take ownership of the initiatives, increasing their long-term sustainability;

c)   Several external partners are actively involved in supporting (or are being recruited to support) the venture financially, politically and in kind.

✓   Model 2- Hybrid non-profit enterprises (Tcherneva, 2012; Salavou & Manolopoulos, 2019):

a)   As in Model 1 ventures, goods/services are delivered to populations that have been excluded or under-tended by traditional markets , but the notion of making (and reinvesting) a profit is not totally out of the question;

b)   Sooner or later, the founding entrepreneur - or histeam - usually develops a marketing plan to ensure that the poor or otherwise disadvantaged canaccess the product or service being provided;

c)   The company is able to recover part of its costs through the sale of goods and services, often identifying new markets;

d)   To maintain activities and meet the unmet needs of poor or marginalized clients, the entrepreneur mobilizes funds from public, private and/or philanthropic organizations in the form of donations, loans or, in more rare cases, quasi equity investments.

✓   Model 3 - Social Business Enterprises(Marshall, 2011; Salavou & Manolopoulos, 2019):

a)   The entrepreneur configures theenterprise as a business with the specific mission of driving social and/or environmentaltransformation;

b)   Profits are generated, but the main objective is not to maximize financial returns to shareholders, but to financially benefit low-income groups and increase social investment through reinvestment, allowing them to reach and serve more people;

c)   The entrepreneur seeks investors interested in combining financial and social returns;

d)   The opportunities for financing and sizing the company can be significantly greater because social enterprises can more easily take on debt and equity.

CHAPTER 2

SOCIALINNOVATION

Social innovation is about applying the concepts of innovation to the implementation of social entrepreneurship. Dufays (2019), takes an integrated approach to the social innovation process with the implementation phases of social entrepreneurship. This chapter will therefore develop the concepts of innovation, in a comprehensive way, whose application in social entrepreneurship is made when defining the solution and planning the activities. The Austrian Joseph Schumpeter, one of the most important economists of the 20th century, defined "the entrepreneur" as an individual who reforms or revolutionizes the "creative destructive" process of capitalism, through the development of new technology or the improvement of an old one ; individuals, agents of change in the economy. This thinking has formed the basis for the concept of innovation.

The concept of innovation is still contested by some authors as confusing and ambivalent (Adams, Bessant & Phelps, 2006; Bilali, 2018). In the literature innovation is approached as a process, theory, policy, strategy, system and/or indicator. Cited by Bilali, (2018) according to the authors, Stummer, Guenther and Kock, "innovations can be categorized according to (a) the type of innovation (product, service, process, market), (b) dimension (objective or subjective), (c) scope of change (radical, incremental, reapplied) or (d) how the innovation was created (closed or open)".

2.1. TYPES OF INNOVATION

An innovation is the implementation of a new or significantly improved product (good or service), process, new marketing method, or new organisational method, in business practices, workplace organisation or external relations (OECD, 1997). According to the Oslo Manual (OECD, 1997)innovation activities are scientific, technological, organisational, financial and commercial steps that lead, or are intended to lead, to the implementation of innovations. Some innovation activities are in themselves innovative, others are not new activities, but are necessary for the implementation of innovations. Innovation activities also relate to R&D (research and development) which is not directly related to the development of a specific innovation. For the group, R&D is the construction and testing of a prototype, if its main objective is to make further improvements. A prototype is an original model (or a test situation) that includes all the technical characteristics and functions of the new product or process. Acceptance of a prototype often means the end of the experimental development phase and the start of a new phase in the innovation process. Someexamples of innovation activities are

a) Market research;

b) Acquisition of technology and know-how and knowledge;

c) Purchase of machinery, equipment and other capital goods;

d) Installation of equipment and engineering;

e) Tests and evaluations;

f) Changes in procedures;

g) Training to update innovation.

The Oslo Manual (1997) isfollowed to define the types of innovation:

a) Product innovations;

b) Process innovations;

c) Organisational innovations;

d) Marketing innovations.

Which differ somewhat from Schumpeter 's types of innovation (Yezersky, 2007):

a) New products;

b) Newproductionmethods ;

c) New sources of supply;

d) Exploring new markets;

e) New ways to organise business

Product innovation is the introduction of a new or significantly improved good or service in terms of its expected characteristics or uses. Significant improvements are included in technical specifications, components and materials, embedded software, ease of use or other functional features.

Process innovation is the implementation of a new or significantly improved method of production or distribution. It includes significant changes in techniques, equipment and/or software.

Marketing innovation is the implementation of a new marketing method with significant changes in product design or packaging, product positioning, promotion or pricing.

Organisational innovation is the implementation of a new organisational method in the company's business practices, in the organisation of its workplace or in its external relations.

2.2. INNOVATION PROCESS

According to Johnson (2011) the objective of an innovation system can be, (a) development, (b) dissemination and (c) use of innovation. The author classifies the innovation system as a technological, technical and socio-technical system. The (a) knowledge, (b) learning and (c) interactivity between the actors is what gives rise to the "innovation systems".

Johnson (2011), in his study on functions of the innovation system, addresses that in an innovation system , aninnovator is needed ,so that knowledge is transferred, and an entrepreneur to identify and select commercially viable innovations and bring them to market. The author (apud Bijker, 1995), uses this thought to define the innovation process, whichconsists in the variation and selection of three factors:

✓ First, the relevant social routers identify a variety of problems, based on perceived functional failures or presumptive anomalies, some of which are selected for further attention.

✓ Secondly, a variety of solutions are generated and some of these solutions generate new artifacts.

✓ And third, one artefact becomes dominant over all relevant social groups, partly as a result of the ability of one relevant social group to convince the other groups of the superiority of its problem definition and resulting artefact.

The Oslo Manual (1997) also considers the systemic approach to innovation processes and specifies three processes that interact in the innovation process:

✓ knowledge creation process;

✓ process of knowledge dissemination and

✓ process of applying knowledge

Johnson (2011) considers that research and experience are importantinputs to the innovation process .The author analyses the relationship between actors in the innovation process,according to Hakansson's factors of importance :

✓ Interactions with companies that have knowledge in other areas can generate technical issues and new knowledge to solve them;

✓ The evaluation and acceptance of a new technology or product depends on the support of several actors;

✓ Companies often need to complement their resources with those of others.

In his literature reviewJohnson (2011) identifies two direct functions of the innovation process:

a) Identify problems;

b) Resolve the problems identified.

And eight supportfunctions :

a) Provide incentives for companies to engage in innovative work;

b) Provide resources;

c) To influence the direction in which actors employ their resources, to generalise innovation or to achieve it more with the resources used;

d) Recognising the growthpotential of innovation;

e) Facilitate the exchange of information and knowledge;

f) Stimulate/createmarket;

g) Reducing social uncertainty, i.e. uncertainty about how others will act and react;

h) Neutralizing resistance to change, which can arise in society, with theintroduction of technology (legitimizinginnovation and the activities of the system before society).

Problems can be identified by (a) identifying system*bottlenecks* ,technology or relationship bottlenecks (functional failures), (b) lack of complementary stages, (c) outstanding reverse results, (d) imbalances. And the solution of problems will result in a new product or new technology, which will create new knowledge. Resources for innovation are (a)financial, (b)skills and (c) relationships.

In an innovation system the exchange of information and knowledge allows (a) feedback between system performance and targets for dissemination of the technology or product on the market,(b) coordination of the different areas ofactivities, (c) promotion of cooperation betweenactors and (d) division of labour between actors.

According to the Oslo Manual (OECD, 1997) innovation processes differ greatly from sector to sector in terms of (a) development, (b) rate of technological change, (c) interactions and access to knowledge, (d) organisational structures and (e) institutional factors.

2.3. THEORIES OF INNOVATION

Innovation theories emerge from the evolution of growth theories and are introduced into academia through a debate on the role of innovation in the competitiveness of enterprises and countries. With the evolution of innovation theories, researchers no longer see innovation as a discovery process butas a learning process.

The Evolutionary Theory of Economic Change by Richard Nelson and Sydney Winter described by Mytelka and Smith (2002) is based on the idea that innovation is shaped by the company through crisis-oriented research programmes . The authors induce thought, that as procedures fail in the face of economic and technological change, firms seek alternatives in experimental learning processes. This learning occurs in specific institutional contexts, i.e. , systemic environments shaped by regulation, law, political cultures, the "rules of the game" of economic institutions and political actions. According to this theory, the innovation process presents a non-linear model , whosenature is characterized by the effect of the uncertainties and unpredictability of this process and a dynamic impact, whose dynamism results from the learning of agents, interactions and process patterns . Thus the theory predicts that different actors would do different things. They would see opportunities differently. And they would classify differentlywhat everyone saw. The theory is acriticism of neoclassicism. But it was Nathan Rosenberg 's ideas, significantly changed the understanding of innovation; through Schumpeter 's critique of innovation and ideas for post-innovation improvements, which brought the concept of "adoption" and a complexity in the distinction between innovation and diffusion, but highlighted the idea of learning.

Yezersky (2007) presents the assumptions of the General Theory of Innovation (TGI), which is based on:

✓ Any product or service (process) is a system: itmeans that each product or service represents the union of parts or procedures connected to each other in order to add valueto customers. No individual element of a system can deliver the same value alone;

✓   Systems (products, services, industries) evolve:systems evolve over time to adapt to change, according tocustomer needs and wishes;

✓   Systems evolve in the prevailing direction: the course of a system's evolution coincides with the delivery ofincreasing performance , requiring fewer resources to deliver that performance.

The predominant direction of evolution can be expressed as the ratio of thesum of the functions of a system (a performance mode) to the sum of connections that the system needs to establish in order to obtain the necessary resources to achieve functionality. The relationship between function and connection is called Coefficient (C) of Freedom (any function enables a system and makes it freer, while any connection increases its dependency and decreases freedom), incorporates the business, a worldwide concept of value. The higher the coefficient, the higher the valuedelivered for a product or service.

$$C\ liberdade = \frac{\sum Fun\varsigma\tilde{o}es}{\sum Conex\tilde{o}es}$$

The postulate of the General Theory of Innovation (GTI), firstdefined in 1988,concludes that, (a) systems do not evolve randomly,(b) the evolutionary cycle of all systems, regardless of their specific nature, is governed by the same set of natural laws, which are completely independentof human will and desire. The natural law governing the process of revolution (growth, expansion) of various systems states that "the direction of an evolution of the system coincides with a continually increasing degree of freedom ofthe environment of this system" and istherefore entitled Law of a Growing Degree of Freedom.

Rogers'Theory of Dissemination of Innovation determines the adoptionof specific behavioursand to decide which components will require additional effort for dissemination to occur .It originated in 1962 in communication to explain how, over time, an idea or product gains momentum and spreads (or spreads) across a specific population or social system. The conclusion of this thinking is that people, as part of a social system, adopt a new idea, behavior or product. Adoption means that a person does something different than what he or she previously did (i.e. buy or use a new product, acquire and perform a new behaviour, etc.).

People do not adopt an innovation simultaneously.Researchers have found that people who adopt an innovation early have different characteristics than people who adopt an innovation later. For this reason, this theory analyses the characteristics of the target audience thatwill help or hinder the adoption of theinnovation and focuses on strategies to be used toimprove dissemination.

Innovators: they are people who want to be the first to experience innovation. People who are willing to take risks and are usually the first to develop new ideas. Very little or nothing needs to be done to attract this population. The literature presents at least five categories of adoptionstages. The dissemination is done in the stage where a person adopts an innovation:

✓ Pioneer users:these are people who represent opinion leaders. They like leadership roles and embrace opportunities for change. They are already aware of the need for change and are therefore very comfortable adopting new ideas. Strategies to attract this population include instruction manuals and implementation information sheets;

✓ Initial majority: these people are rarely leaders, but they adopt new ideas before thelate majority. Strategies to attract this population include success stories and evidence of innovation effectiveness;

✓ Late majority:these people are skeptical of change and will only adopt an innovation after it has been tried by the majority . Strategies to attract this population include information on how many other people have experienced the innovation and successfully adopted it;

✓ Latecomers:these people are bound by tradition and very conservative. They are very sceptical about change and are the most difficult group to accept. Strategies to attract this population include statistics, appeals to fear and pressure from people from other adoption groups.

There are five factors that influence the adoption of innovation ,and partially determine whether the diffusion of a new activity will occur and are: relative advantage, compatibility, complexity, experimentation and observability.

✓ Relative advantage - The degree to which an innovation is seen as better than the idea, programme or product it replaces;

✓ Compatibility - the degree to which an innovation is perceived as compatible with existing values, past experiences and the needs of potential adopters;

✓ Complexity - the degree to which an innovation is perceived as difficult to understand and use;

✓ Experimentation - the degree to which innovation can be tested and modified before an adoption commitment is made;

✓ Observability - the degree to which the results of innovation are visible to others.

Sanson-Fisher (2004) in its diffusion model for clinical innovations presents three components, (a) communication style, (b) decision   making processand (c) social context.

✓ Communication style: The communication channels used to convey information about clinical practice include research publications, databases (e.g. the Cochrane database), the mass media, participation in lectures and workshops, visits by interest groups and videos or audio tapes;

✓ The decision-making process: the dissemination model, postulates five stages in the decision-making process :

    o   Researchers gain knowledge about the proposed clinical change;

    o   The individual clinician is convincedof the advantages of innovation ;

    o   The clinician engages in activities that will lead to a choice about adopting or rejecting innovation;

    o   Innovation is incorporated into the clinician's daily activity;

    o   The clinician seeks reinforcement over the innovation decision.

✓ The social context:the systems most likely to respond easily and quickly to innovation are those with a culture of creativity and innovation, a relatively flat hierarchical system and strong leadership that is committed to change. In contrast, the health care system has a hierarchical model, with distinct organizational structures for each professional group. It is a bureaucratic system and it will be necessary to change some aspects of clinical activity .

Sanson-Fisher (2004) identified   ofdissemination theory , (a) some stages ofuser categories are not as explicit in public healthprogrammes , (b) it does not promote a participatory approach to the adoption ofa public health programme, (c) it does not take into account the resources of an individual or social support to adopt the new behaviour.

CHAPTER 3

IMPLEMENTATION STRUCTUREOF SOCIAL ENTREPRENEURSHIP

The social entrepreneurship model should not be confused with the implementation structure of the social entrepreneurship model . Although the former influences the latter. Inpractice, the social entrepreneurship model is about the selection ofthe social business model and has already been presented, while the implementation structure of social entrepreneurship is about the stages of developmentof the social business. There is no consensus on the stages of development presented, some authors or institutions follow the logic of a business plan, but others follow thelogic of the development of the main concepts.

Stanford University Social Entrepreneurship Hub, presents an implementation model with the following steps:

The following is the structure developed by for a social entrepreneurship plan (Ashoka, 2011) and ECLAC (1997) to implement their social projects:

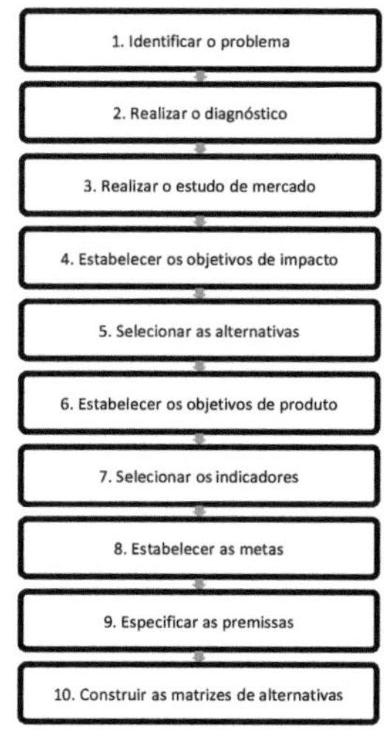

Source: *Ashoka*   Source: ECLAC

Dulays (2019) presented a model for implementing social entrepreneurship integrated into the social innovation process, with the following characteristics:

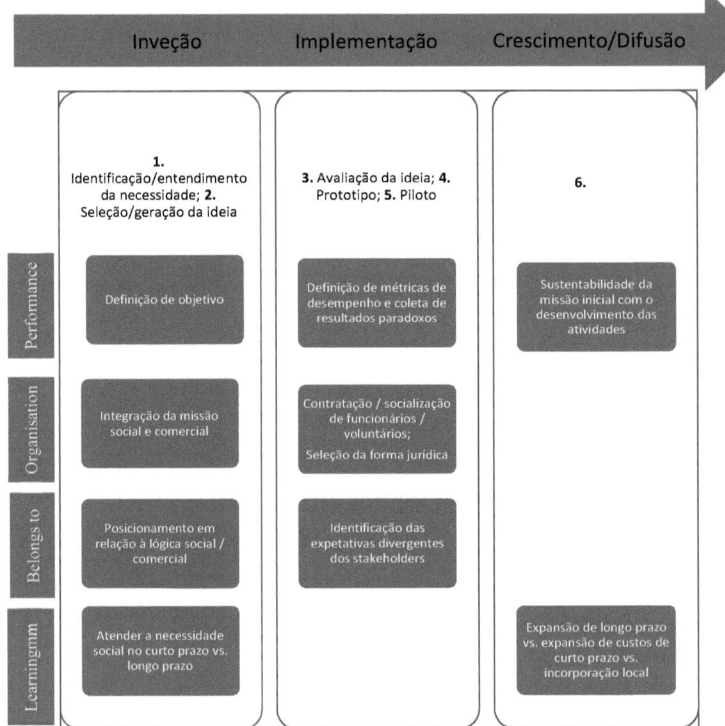

Source: Dufays, 2019

Regardless of the different phases, the different structures apply the same concepts. Concepts, which distinguish a social entrepreneurship solution fromother types of solutions, such as the social problem, the solution, the financing of the solution and theevaluation of the solution .

3.1. DEVELOPING THE PROBLEM

The main objective of the social entrepreneur is to create a positive social impact on society and his mission is based on attacking important and neglected problems toresult in positive externalities.

A problem is characterised by being:

✓ Important - it affects a large number of people negatively or has extremely negative consequences for a small segment of society. A critical problem negatively affects a large number of people.

✓ Neglected - not being addressed by different social actors (public or private - governments, markets or civil society). This is because the problem is ignored by society, either the solution is expensive or the solutions found are not effective.

✓ Positive externalities - solving the problem creates more value for society than the value generated by current market mechanisms.

The "Problem Tree" is a tool that structures the analysis of problems, helping to understand the anatomy of the problem in identifying its causes and effects. In this methodology, the problem is seen as a tree with roots and ramifications (causes and effects) that can be schematically organised (ECLAC, 1997; Buvinich,1999).

The Tree of Problems allows, (a) making a representation of reality, enabling the correct formulation of objectives; (b) breaking down the problem into its different components, giving strength to its action; (c) attacking the root causes of the problems; (d) discussing and clarifying the causes and effects of theproblems and understanding why a specific problem persists; (e) establish the type of additional information needed to continue building the best solution; (f) understand the challenges that may be encountered in developing the solution, such as key resources or relevant partnerships; (g) understand, in a logical way, which are the fields of action with superior comparative advantage. In the figure below we can analyse the constituent parts of the problem tree:

Figure 4: Problem tree

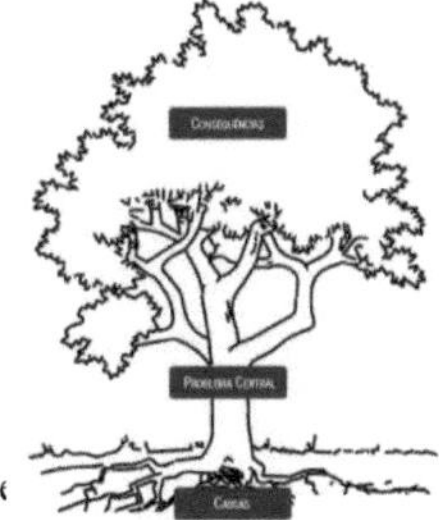

The steps to build the 1997; Dib-Ferreira 2010; Lacerda Botelho & Colussi, 2017):

Source: Lacerda, Botelho and Colussi,

✓ Definition of the central problem;

✓ Identification of effects;

✓   Identification of causes.

1st Defining the Central Problem: identification of a "deficiency or deficit in society, the " 5W2H" problem associated with "brainstorming"is used to define the problem. Then any creative technique of group discussion can be usedto generate consensus on the common statement of the problem. The problem should always be defined by actors involved in the context. The problem identified must be real, and presented as a negative state that directly or indirectly affects most of the actors involved.

2. Identify the effects: Listall the consequences that followthe central problem and then relate these and officially reported, reported or studied facts.

3 .Identify the causes: list all the problems preceding the central problem and then relate them to each other, generating a hierarchy of problems until it reaches the root problem, thus defining the causes of the problem. The causes of the central problem should be described objectively as a negative present situation and not the lack of a certain situation. For example, the problem is not "the lack of money for street vendors to take their children to school", but "(a) the high cost of school for them or (b) thelow level of schoolingoftheir family carers" .

3.2. DEVELOPING THE SOLUTION

The value propositionholds out the promise of the value that the new idea is intended to offer. The value to the customer is the difference between the perceived benefits and costs of a product or service. And it is noticed as positive when the performance is superior, to the total cost of the customer, or to the benefits with the current solutions, in the case of social problems. Value is created when there is a relationship between the benefit offered by the idea and the needs of the target audience.

The value proposition is presented in an *Elevator Speech*, short statement of one or two sentences of about 10 seconds duration. The statement should be very clear about the tangible results for the public using the solution created. And it should be results-oriented, highlighting the social value or the value of the social or economic business that the solution proposes on the market (Konrath, 2012).

To measure the performance of the solution, the value proposition should be tested withthe target audience, suppliers, internal staff and all other *stakeholders*. Osterwalder, Pigneur, Bernarda and Smith (2014) define "value proposition as the set of products and services that create value for a specific customer segment.

The value proposition serves to:

    ✓   To present the business to *stakeholders;*

    ✓   Promote anddisseminate social business;

✓ Use inofficial businesscommunications (letter writing and meetings with decision makers should be inspired by the Value Proposition).

The Social Entrepreneur who is seeking partnerships and affirming his idea, should communicate his value propositionin institutional events, groups of friends and informal conversations, advertisements and propaganda and in the hiring or training of a new collaborator.

The type of value proposition is based on the type of solution and this determines how the proposal will be declared:

✓ New Solution - meets a new need. Nobody is facing this concrete problem;

✓ Solution to improve performance -it allows toimprove, to be the best;

✓ Solution to adapt to the client - allowsaccess when the problem is "unableto meet a need due to lack of access";

✓ Easy-to-use solution - allows you to adapt something to be easier to obtain when the problem is "not being able to obtain something effectively";

✓ Solution to empower the customer - enable the public to participate in the delivery of objectives;

✓ Solution for social awareness - makes the public part ofthe movement;

✓ Price reduction solution - allowing access by reducing the price when the problem is related to lack of access foreconomic reasons.

Someexamples of valueproposition are given:

✓ *Uber*: Just order inthe app and a car will come directly to you: it's easy, it's always ready when you need it and with options from economy to luxury.

✓ *Netflix*: Your next story, now. Watch where you want, cancel when you want.

✓ *Mozabikes*: Providing rural Mozambicanswith a safe, cheap and efficientmeans of transport;

✓ *ADRA*: To contribute to democratic and sustainable rural development, socially and environmentally just, and to the process of national reconciliation and peace in Angola; *Omunga*: To promote, disseminate and monitor throughout the national territory, policies for children and youth that guarantee and exercise their rights and duties.

Thedevelopmentstages ofthe ValueProposition are:

✓ Converting the problem tree into a goal tree;

✓ Select the solution;

✓ Selecting interested parties

✓ Search forreferences in bestpractices (benchmarking);

✓ Define the implementation activities of the solution.

1° From causes to objectives: totransform the problem tree into an objective tree , it is necessary to rewrite all the negative situations into desired or positive situations. That is, todescribe the objectives in an explicit and structured way, and to identify the linked or related objectives in a logical order.

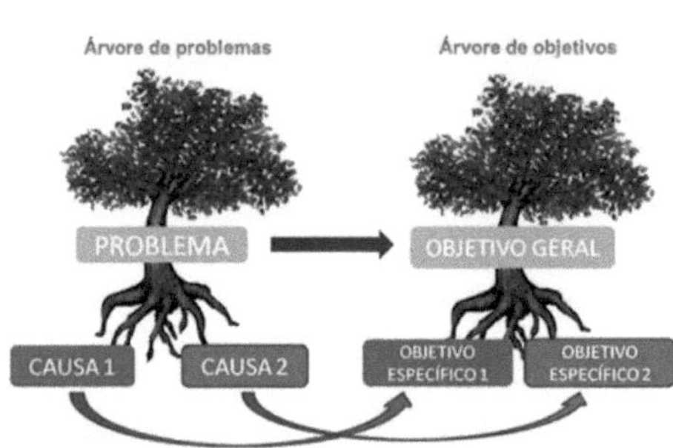

Figure 6: The problem tree and the Objectives tree

Source: Lacerda, Botelho & Colussi, 2017

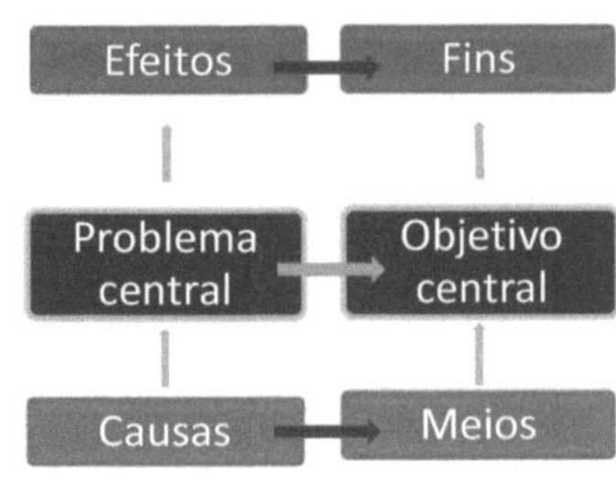

Figure 5: From the problem tree to the Objectives tree

Source: own elaboration

Theselectionsteps ofthe solution are

a)   Select a root cause of the problem on which to apply the solution. When the action of the problem is converted from a negative to a positive action ,the objectiveis formed , which is the solution. If there is more than one root cause, the one that most influences the existence ofthe social problem analysed or the one that offers the most viability of resolutionis chosen ;

b)   Identify who or what is most affected by the problem. This will be the target audience of the proposal;

c)   Make a list of interests or motivations for solving the problem.These will be the performance measures of the proposal, which willbe analysed as results of the solution, generating the social impact.

The value propositionstatement expresses made up ofthe following elements: social objective, target audienceand social impact.

Figure 7: Value Proposition Statement

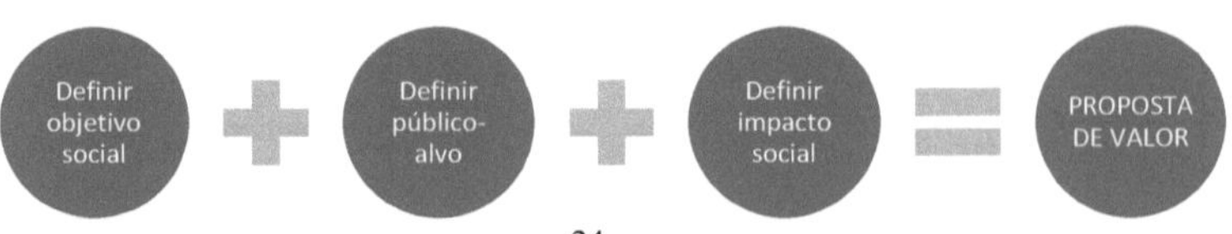

24

Source: own elaboration

To select interested parties is necessary:

1º.   Make a listof accessible skills and resources for solution development and identify the available parts;

2º.   Make a list of indispensable and inaccessible skills and resources for solution development and identifypotential partners;

3º.   Identify partners by asking the following questions: (a) Who benefits from the solution? (b) Who is interested in the solution created?(c) Who do youwant to help and (d)Who can prevent the solution from being implemented?

Table 5 below will help to identify the best partners.

Table 2: Selection of *Stakeholders*

Who	Contributions	Winnings	Expected values

Source: UDI-ASocial Entrepreneurship, NOVA SBE, 2018

The questions below have helped tomake a good, benchmarking solution:

- ✓ Who else faces this problem?
- ✓ What other solutions are there and what are they doing?
- ✓ What works and what doesn't?
- ✓ What are the average results and impact achieved? Best in class and average?
- ✓ What are the best practices in industry and other areas?
- ✓ What is the best competing solution?
- ✓ Why is my solution different?
- ✓ My solution is 10 times better?

Table 6 below will help to analyse the solutions identified in search of the best performance for the new solution.

Table 3: *Benchmarking*

Solutions	Causes addressed		Results +	Results -

Source: UDI-ASocial Entrepreneurship, NOVA SBE, 2018

To define the implementation activities of the solution it is necessary to follow the following steps:

✓   List the main activities to fulfil the results of the solution;

✓   Define for each activity, the key sustainable and innovative resources required. Some types of resources can be identified in table 7 below.

Table 4: KeyResources

Structure	Knowledge	Human	Relational
Constructions,	Brand,	Technicians,	Capital stock,
Transport,	Skills,	Managers,	Credibility,
Vehicles,	Patents,	Volunteers,	Share,
Machines,	Copyrights,	Administrative.	Commitment,
Material,	Partnerships,		Social network.
Equipment, etc.	Data/Bases, etc.		

Source: UDI-ASocial Entrepreneurship, NOVA SBE, 2018

✓   Not all activities need to be managed by the same entity. The solution will usually involve and mobilise resources from different organisations. To design the solution is to identify the main activities, make them innovative and define the main resources needed for this. The following questions will help to define the best activities:

✓   Can the solution reduce operational costs?

✓   Can the solution be more efficient?

✓   Could the solution be more innovative?

✓   Is there full use of available resources?

✓   Are you empowering your customers and users?

✓   Is the initiative sustainable in the long term?

When all the activities have been created they can be presented in anaction plan using the 5W2H model , which is a quality management tool. The action plan is essential to plan and evaluate the activities to implement the solution.

Table 5: 5W2H technique

	Questions	Problems	Solutions
1-	What / What	...is that the problem?	...will it be done? What is the action?
2-	Why / Why	...occurs?	...has this solution been defined?
3-	When / When	... (since when) occurs?	...will it be done?
4-	Where / Where	...ishe?	...will it be deployed?
5-	Who / Who	...are you involved?	...will you be responsible?
1-	How / How	...did the problem arise?	...will it be implemented?
2- Costs	How Much It	...have this problem?	...this solution?

Source: adapted https://slideplayer.com.br/slide/5614817/

<h1 style="text-align:center">CHAPTER 4</h1>
<h1 style="text-align:center">SOCIAL IMPACT ASSESSMENT</h1>

Social Impact Assessment is the process of measuring change that non-profit organizations, programmes and projects create (Mulgan, 2010, 2008). Social Impact is the change brought about by an organization, program or initiative to the well-being of individuals or communities, and can be reflected in economic, social and environmental impacts. Impact can be measured by looking at reducing transaction costs; reducing social vulnerability; and increasing individual and family assets. Somesocial impact measurement instrumentsare influenced and adapted from theprivate sector and take the quantitative approach to measuring the social impact created, (Arvidson, Lyon, McKay & Moro ,2013). *Philanthrocapitalist*movementsapply business methods to the social sector(Bishop & Green, 2008).Quantitative or qualitative indicators are almost always usedtomeasuresocial impact.

4.1. EVALUATION BY INDICATORS

According to Ferreira, Cassiolato and Gonzalez (2009), "The indicator is a measure, of a quantitative or qualitative order, endowed with particular significance and used to organise and capture the relevant information of the elements making up the object of observation". It is a methodological resource that provides empirical information on the evolution of the observed aspect.

The indicators can be classified into

    ✓ Effort indicators;

    ✓ Result indicators.

The English term *drivers*, expresses the indicatorof effort and *outcomes*, indicators of results.

A measurement system should be formed by result and effort indicators.

    ✓ For each outcome indicator, one or more effort indicators should be chosen;

    ✓ The mixing of effort indicators with outcome indicators is the key to structuring a balanced system.

Table 6 below presents the attributes that the indicator shouldhave in order to be considered as such. Table 7 shows the types of indicators and table 8 below shows how the indicators are classified.

Table 6: Attributes of institutional indicators

Utility	The indicator should communicate the intention of the objective. There should be a relationship between the indicator and the objective.

Representativeness	The indicator should faithfullyrepresent what is to be measured. The indicator should be close or comprehensive in relation to the objective.
Methodological reliability	Methods of collecting and processing the indicator must be reliable, previously disclosed or accepted. Avoid methods that are understood or known only to those who create them.
Reliability of source	The source must provide the indicator accurately.
Availability	The data needed to calculate the indicator should be possible to collect.
Economic	The cost-benefitratio to obtain the indicator should be favourable
Simplicity of communication	The indicator should be easy to understand for the general public. Use clear indicators that prove, financial sustainability of the model; Impact and that it is possible to compare results (assess competitiveness).
Measurement	Measures to monitor and compare the indicator throughout the action planshould be created
News	The indicator should be obtained in real time or the information should be updated
Sensitivity	It is necessary to analyse whether the indicator is sensitive to any variable in order to controlit,

Source: Own elaboration

Table 7: Types of indicators

Type of Indicator	Meaning	Example
Effectiveness	Itmeasures the impactof actions in context, adding value.	Number of students who became involved in social projects in the community after the course.
Effectiveness	It measures how much was delivered of what was needed.	Number of students programmed per number ofstudents who have completed the course.
Efficiency	It measures the relationship between the services delivered and the resources spent.	Number of students who completed the course for thetotalcost of the course.
Implementation	It measures the quantity executed.	Number of students who have completed the course.
Inputs	Measures the amount of inputs or put's spent.	Total cost of the course.

Source: Adapted from FNQ, 2012

Table 8: Effort and outcome indicators

Type	Effort Indicators	Performance Indicators
Indicators	Inputs Implementation Efficiency	Effectiveness Effectiveness
Description	It measures the cause before the effect happens; It serves to verify that plans linked to critical success factors are being fulfilled; Suitable for measuringactions.	It measures the effect after a certain time; It serves to verify that the objectives are being achieved; Suitable for measuring the achievement of objectives.

Source: FNQ, 2012

The dashboard is a tool that helps the selection of indicators and the practical construction of a performance measurement system. Critical successfactor(FCS) is a challenge, obstacle or constraint that, if not overcome, will prevent the achievement of the goal (Pinto & Prescott, 1998; Rabechini ,

Carvalho & Laurindo, 2002). An expected result for a goal will only be considered achieved if the outcome indicator goal is also met, and this will depend on the critical success factors, which will only be considered exceeded if the effort indicator goals are met.

Table 9: Structure of a Scoreboard

Action	Objective	Critical success factor	Result indicator	Effort Indicator
...	...	...	...	...

Source: Own elaboration

The interpretation of the indicators deserves special attention, as it may be responsible for the success or failure ofthe project. The following is an example of the Quality Foundationof Brazil with thenecessary elements for the correct calculation of the indicators.

Table 10: Indicator Findings

Element	Example
Indicator	Infant mortality rate
Target	12/1000 (12 deaths of children up to one year per 1000 live births)
Periodicity of verification	monthly
Maximum time limit for verification	10th of each month
Responsibility for verification	João da Silva
Data source	Health system
Form of data collection	Manual collection of the amount of children born alive, from the health system.
How to calculate the indicator	Calculate the number of deaths of children up to one year old in the month among the residents of the municipality=>numerator. Determine the number of children born alive in the municipality in the month => denominator. Divide the numerator by the denominator and multiply by 1000
What the indicator shows	Quality of nutrition and hygiene conditions of the population and the state health system.
What can cause a less-than-target result	Deficiencies in the care of pregnant women, in the nutrition and hygiene conditions of the homes, in the health care system...
What is the impact of a less-than-target result?	Negative commotion from citizens and dissatisfaction with the state government.

Source: FNQ, 2012

4.2. SOCIAL IMPACT ASSESSMENT INDICATOR

In social projects, the Theory of Changeprovides an organizing principle and with other social sectorevaluation structures , such as thelogic model, programme model and evaluation plan, ofa robust evaluationprogramme.

The programme model benefits the theory of change by including significant details on how to design and . The programme model should have high implementation value, which means that it should support the implementation of the programme on site and in theteam.

The logicmodel benefits the theory of change byincluding significant details for monitoring and evaluating a programme. It includes inputs (financial, human and other resources needed for an effort), services and activities, outputs (tangible products or deliveries created as a result of activities) and time-sequenced results.

The evaluation plan benefits the theory of change by providing the roadmap for measurement. Often built on alogicalmodel . the evaluationplan defines the specific process measures and indicators of success that need to be collected in order to test the theory ofchange. At its core, changetheory challenges us to articulate our assumptions and how we create the change I want in and for our target population .

Thus, in addition to the above structures, a theory of change must include:

✓   The need to address the root causes of the problem;

✓   Beliefs about the drivers of change;

✓   Factors affecting success, whether positive or negative.

The process of developing a theory of change:

✓   Create an agreement on how change happens, what is needed to get there and what defines success;

✓   Help to challenge and clarify the underlying logic of the connection between strategies and results;

✓   Clarify the context and factors affecting success,

✓   Determine what level of change stakeholders can reasonably expect with the resources at their disposal.

The value chain or impact chain is an evaluation structure (Roche, 2000). The elements of itare shown below in figure 8 and exemplified in table 11 below.

Figure 8: Impact chain

Source: UDIA-Social Entrepreneurship NOVA SBE, 2018

Table 11: Evaluation structure

N	Action (activities)	Input (resources)	Output (benefits)	Out comes (results)	Impact (changes)
1	Conduct environmental awareness campaigns with vendors	Illustrated material, volunteers, Clothing.	100 sellers involved	100 environmentally aware salespeople	Reduction in malaria deaths.
2	Carry out tree planting campaign	30 tree seedlings .	30 trees planted	Wooded market environment	
3	Carry out a waste collection campaign	Cleaningmaterial/equipment.	100 sellers involved	Clean market environment	

Source: own elaboration

✓ *Inputs* or resources invested in the activity: these are the means by which the business will achieve the intended social impact;

✓ *Outputs* or immediate results: are the direct and tangible products obtained through the activity, such as number of customers,units ofproductssold or volume of credit granted;

✓ *Other foods*, or medium and long-term results: this is the change generated in the lives of people exposed to business activity, such as income generation, reduction of vulnerability or increase in social capital;

✓ Social Impact: significant or lasting change in people's lives achieved through a given action or series of actions.

SROI, *Social Retur on Investment*, is an internationally recognised methodology that determines the social return of an intervention/social organisation by comparing the value of the resources invested in it with the value of the social impact generated.

The unit of measurement used to calculate the social return on investment is currency, as it is the measure in which a large part of the components of the analysis are already valued (all the accounting data that reveal the resources consumed) and as it is the easiest way to translate the subjective utility of a benefit to a beneficiary.

The SROI ratio is obtained by dividing the value of the economic and social impact, translated into monetary terms, and the net present value of the investments made. A ratio of 2:1 indicates that for every 1Kz invested in an activity, the return is 2Kz in social value. (Everis, 2015). The formula is as follows:

$$SROI = \frac{\textbf{Soma dos Valores para comunidade (tangível e intangível)}}{\textbf{Tempo + custo do investimento}}$$

The 7 SROI principles are:

1°.   Involve *stakeholders* in the processes of measuring and quantifying social value;

2°.   Understand the changes generated, recognizing both positive and intentional changes as well as negative and unintentional effects of the activity;

3°.   Valuing what matters, monetising the value of unquoted benefits/losses in the market;

4°.   Only include what is relevant, so that a true picture of the activity is presented, from which *stakeholders* can draw reasonable conclusions about its impact;

5°.   Only claim the value created by the activity, taking into account the impact generated by other external factors;

6°.   Be transparent, demonstrating proof of the robustness and honesty of the analysis;

7°.   Verify the results throughan external authorship or inspection certification.

4.3. GROWTH STRATEGIES

The ideaof growing entrepreneurial projects and initiatives is compatible with the need to increase social impact, i. e. once the social problem is identified, resources are mobilized to solve the problem. In a first phase, social initiative may not be able to affect every segment of the vulnerable target population. However, the extent to which the initiative will think about sustainability and continuity strategies will see an increase in capital, which as a rule is not redistributed to shareholders, but is reinvested in the social business to serve more people. Hence the need for growth. From this perspective, the growth process is linked to the non-conformity of the social entrepreneur who wants to see the social problem solved. This cannot happen if the entrepreneur continues to serve only the same people and in the same geographical unit. So the social entrepreneur has to mobilize more resources in order to expand his or her range of action .

There are basically three reasons why the organisation or initiative should grow:

- ✓ Increase the organization's chances of survival;
- ✓ Increaseefficiency through economies of scale;
- ✓ Enhancing effectiveness by maximising social impact.

The growth process is part of the three phases of a social business life cycle (Sucupira, 2015):

- ✓ Start-up;
- ✓ Growth;
- ✓ Expansion.

Thegrowth of a social innovation occurs when a project reaches the planned level of performance and can be implemented on a larger scale with a view to enhancing social impact (Webb, Kistruck, Ireland, Ketchen,2003). As a social innovation expands, changes in network elements, knowledge, experience and credibility can be observed. However, it is worth noting that not all social innovations have the potential to expand, some are either local or do not wish to expand (Silva, Takahashi & Segatto, 2016). The process of growth of a social innovation can occur in several ways. If it occurs in a pure way we have: *scaling up, scaling out* and *scaling deep.* For Moore and Riddell (2015), this process does not always take place in a pure way, that is, it does not occur purely up, or out or deep, but a mixture .

The types of growth are:

1°.		*Scaling Up* refers to the expansion of a social innovation to enhance its social impact (Silva, Takahashi & Segatto , 2016). Increasing social impact means assisting more people. Thus, *scaling up* can extend its reach, creating complementary services, for example, to attend more people. *Scaling up* tends to imply changes in legislation and public policy making (Bloom & Skloot, 2010 ; Moore & Riddel, 2015).

2°.

Figure 9: Scaling Up Model

▫ Scaling Up

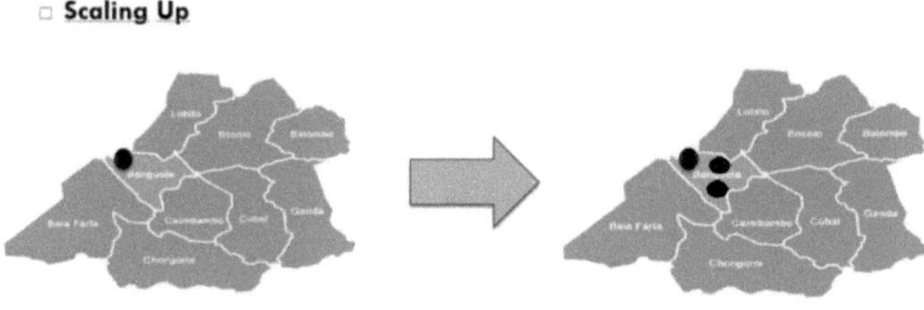

Source: own elaboration

3°.   *Scaling Out* Moore & Riddel , 2015)

Figure 10: Scaling Out Model

▫ Scaling Out

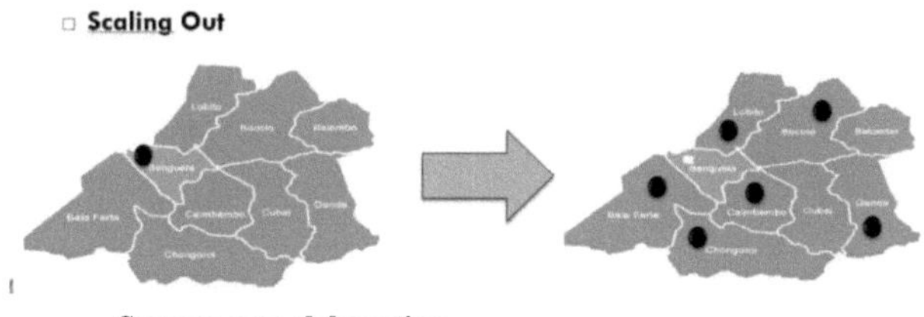

Source: own elaboration

4°.   *Scaling Deep* is the step in expanding a social innovation with the mission of creating social value in its place of origin. It involves cultural changes, personal transformations, changes of beliefs related to the agents involved and the people affected (Moore & Riddel , 2015).

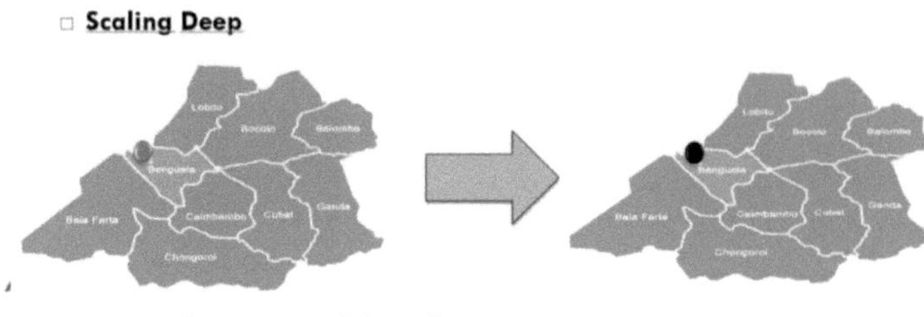

Source: own elaboration

We can then conclude that despite all that has been said about growth and scalability, the social entrepreneur must take care not to deviate from his purpose, mission, values or original vision of his organization, due to the pretension of growth. Growth is the process that lacks financial and human resources; both these and those are scarce. So it is necessary during the growth process not to underestimate quality.

CHAPTER 5

SOCIALFUNDING

Before deciding ona type of financing, the social entrepreneur must know the types of financing existing in their nationalmarket or even the international market , if accessible. The traditional financial market does not usually finance social initiatives. Therefore ,the entrepreneur should look for the social financial market, the one that is integrated into the ecosystem ofsocialentrepreneurship. The capital market reserves specific funds for start-up investments, which areventure capital funds.

5.1. SOURCES OF SOCIALFUNDING

Venturecapital funds (VCFs) are autonomous assets, without legal personality, but with legal personality, belonging to all the holders of the respective units. Under no circumstances are VCFs liable for the debts of the unit-holders, of the entities which carry out the management, deposit and marketing functions, or of other VCFs. Each FCR is managed by a management entity. The management may be exercised by a Venture Capital Company (SCR), by regional development companies and by entities legally qualified to manage closed-end securities investment funds (IAPMEI, 2006) .Theircommon objective is to contributeto the development of innovation, growth and internationalisation strategiesbySMEs and start-ups. This funding is associated with businesses that are starting up, expanding or changing management, inany of these situations there is a very high risk associated with the uncertainty of the project in which the company is, can not be considered as the solution but a possible solution.

The social financial market offers the following financing models for social entrepreneurs:

- ✓   Funding for profit;
- ✓   Non-profit financing;
- ✓   Collaborative funding;
- ✓   Incubator vs. Accelerator;
- ✓   Philanthropicfinanciers;
- ✓   Fundraising.

The following types of funding are available for   profit-making sources:

- a)   *Bootstrapping*: friends,family;
- b)   Collaborative funding;
- c)   Competitions;

d)   Incubators and accelerators;

e)   Empresass, angel individuals with high net worth;

f)   Sales;

g)   Social investors;

h)   Creditors;

i)   Foundations and corporations;

j)   Institutional investors.

Figure 12: The Social Enterprise Funding Eco-System| Forprofits

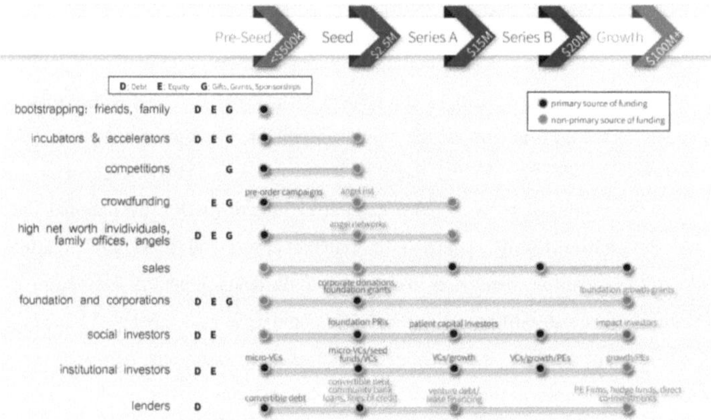

Source: Stanford Business Center for Social Innovation

For non-profitsources there are the following types offunding:

a)   Tax sponsorship andreinforcement (friends, family);

b)   Collaborative funding;

c)   Competitions;

d)   Incubators and accelerators;

e)   Offices, angelindividuals with high net worth ;

f)   Recipe obtained;

g)   Creditors;

h)   Foundations and Corporations.

i)   Government funding.

Figura 13: The Social Enterprise Funding Eco-System Nonprofits

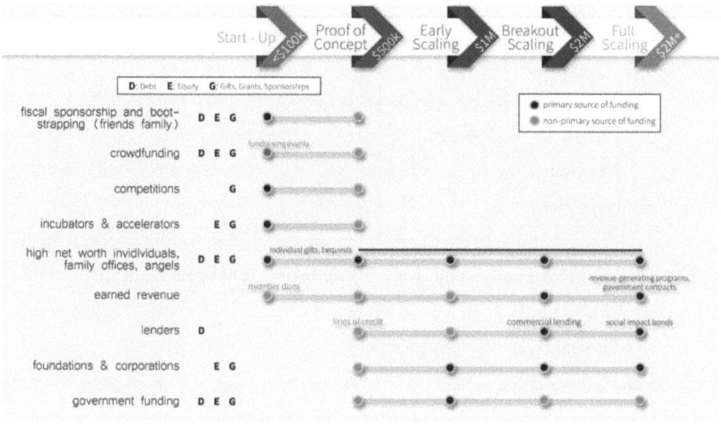

Source: Stanford Business Center for Social Innovation

Crowdfunding is the collective effort of individuals to gather financial support for efforts initiated by others and organisations through the Internet (Stanford University Social Entrepreneurship Hub). This platform uses the following types of funding:

a)   Equity - investors receive a stake in the company;

b)   Debt - investors are reimbursed for their investment over a period of time;

c)   Rewards and philanthropy - investors receive a tangible item or service in exchange for their funds.

Incubators and accelerators are another opportunity for those who are starting a business, todevelop their businessmodeland to engage in fundraising (Stanford University Social Entrepreneurship Hub). See below the characteristics of accelerators and incubators.

Main features of an accelerator:

a)   A definite deadline and rigid structure;

b)   Access to: mentors, services, space, networks and likely investors;

c)   Extremely selective application process for the best programmes;

d)   Microinvestments. Generally, the investment is in exchange forassets of6-8%;

e)   Depending on the programme, one or moreteammembers will be relocated to participate in the programme;

f)   A Demo day for start-ups topresent ideas to investors and media.

Main Features of an Incubator:

a)   No fixed term and loose structure;

b)   Generally access to: advice, services, space, networks, guidance and likely investors;

c)   Extremely selective application process for the best programmes;

d)   They generally ask for a stake in the company, 2-10%;

e)   Depending on the programme, one or moreteammembers will be relocated to participate in the programme;

f)   A possible Demo day for start-ups topresent ideas to investors and media.

For philanthropic funding sources there are the following types of funding:

a) Donations;

b) Philanthropic contributions.

There is no single fundraising model, butthree factors have been proven effective in fundraising :(a) spending money to raise money, (b) going where the money is, and (c) overcoming your fear of asking for money (Jonker, Meehan III, and Iseminger, 2014).Some types of fundraisingare:

a)   Auctions;

b)   Entertainment;

c)   Food trade or convenience;

d)   Antiques dealers;

e)   Community leadership;

f)   Social clubs.

To choose the type of financing, the social entrepreneur must verify at which stage of the life cycle his enterprise is at and whether his social business model is (a) purely philanthropic, (b) purely commercial or (c) hybrid (Emerson, 2003).

Figure 14 below represents the capital flow of the social financing market between suppliers and capital demanders throughout the life cycle of a social enterprise and presents the stages of the life cycle: (a) idea development, (b) pilot, (c) start-up, (d) growth, (e) replication and (f) closure.

Figure 14: Financing Options During the Life Cycle of the Social Enterprise

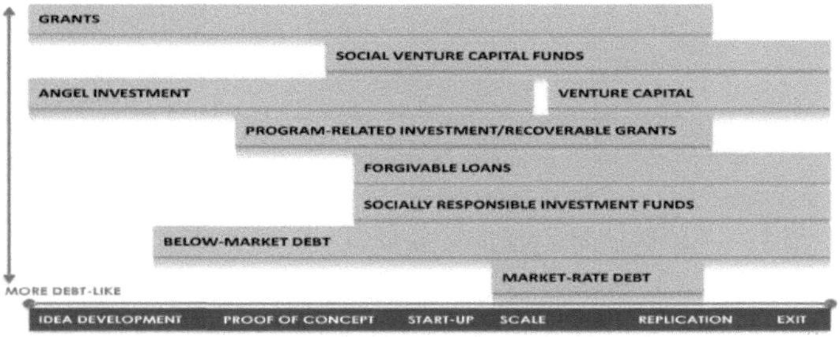

Source: UDIA-Social Entrepreneurship NOVA SBE, 2018

5.2. FINANCING SOCIALENTREPRENEURSHIP IN ANGOLA

There is no public or private institution in the country to finance social initiatives with risk capital or lost funds.Thereare onlypublic and private institutionsusing their social funds to reward social initiatives. However, this is not a programme aimed at entrepreneurship. Therefore, the risk funds available to public and private commercial banks or secondary market investment capital currently only finance entrepreneurial initiatives for profit and the most commonly used models are (a) development programmes and (b) microfinance. We will not address these issues entirely here, since it is outside our scope to deal with entrepreneurship. But since microfinance can be harnessed for profit-making or hybrid social enterprises, we will limit ourselves to developing this topic only.

A series of micro-finance programmes and products used in Angola are presented.

Microcapital, Sociedade de Microcrédito, Lda. is a programmedesigned to facilitate access to credit for people with special difficulties in integrating into the labour market, who are at risk of social exclusion and have a viable business idea. It is a non-bank financial institution supervised by the Angolan National Bank, which aims to provide microcredit to entrepreneurs on an individual or collective basis up to a limit of AKZ 1 million.

The products offered by this institution are the following:

✓ Micro solidarity: credit intended to finance a group of individuals for the development of an activity. A minimum of 6 people and a maximum of 15 people, with a minimum amount of AKZ 50,000.00 and a maximum amount of AKZ 1,000,000.00. Having a maturity of up to 12 months. In terms of repayment the instalment of capital is fixed and has interest. As guarantees a blank promissory note signed by the customer with a pact of completion in favour of the lender and joint guarantee is required.

✓ Very easy: credit for private entrepreneurs on an individual basis when they have needs related to the advance of their salaries, to cope with the fulfilment of personal projects. With a minimum amount of AKZ 100,000.00 and a maximum amount of AKZ 1,000,000.00. With a maturity of up to 3 months. In terms of repayment the instalment of capital is fixed and has interest. As guarantees a blank promissory note subscribed by the customer with a pact of completion in favour of the lenderis required.

✓ Micro 24 hours: credit for private entrepreneurs on an individual basis when they have needs related to the advance of their salaries, to cope with the fulfilment of personal projects. With a minimum amount of AKZ 100. 000.00 and a maximum amount of AKZ 10,000.00. With a maturity of up to 1 month. In terms of repayment the instalment of capital is fixed and has interest. As guarantees a blank promissory note subscribed by the client with a pact of completion in favour of the lenderis required.

✓ Micro travel: credit to finance travel. With a minimum amount of AKZ 50.000,00 and a maximum amount of AKZ 1.000.000,00. With a maturity of up to 6 months. In terms of repayment the instalment of capital is fixed and has interest. As guarantees a blank promissory note subscribed by the customer with a pact to fill in the lender's favouris required.

✓ Micro-enterprise: credit intended to help the growth of small businesses, being individuals or companies. With a minimum amount of AKZ 50,000.00 and a maximum amount of AKZ 1,000,000.00. With a maturity of up to 12 months. In terms of repayment the instalment of capital is fixed and has interest. As guarantees a blank promissory note subscribed by the customer with a pact of completion in favour of the lender anda surety is required. The disbursement is on the account of the supplier.

✓ Micro-farmer: credit to finance the purchase of fertilisers, fertilisers, seeds and agricultural materials, whether private or micro-enterprises. With a minimum amount of AKZ 50,000.00 and a maximum amount of AKZ 1,000,000.00. With a maturity of up to 12 months. In terms of repayment the instalment of capital is fixed and has interest. As guarantees a blank promissory note subscribed by the customer with a pact to fill in the lender's favour is required.

KixiCrédito S.A. was born from a social initiative for women entrepreneurs developed by the *Development Workshop* (DW). Currently it is developed with a micro-credit design program, the interest rate of 4.9% to small economic initiatives, placating the system of mutual guarantees. It has the following products:

✓ Kixisolidario: a credit granted to groups of people who carry out small   income generating activities.   The aim is toincrease working capital to speed up the business of customers. The conditions of access are, groups of 6 to 15 members who live in the same area of residence and have a small activity. The minimum amount conceived is Kz100,000 (ten thousand kwanzas). The payment of the credit is made in 6 (six) months

✓ Kixisolidario reinforced: a credit granted to groups of people who need a capital reinforcement to get their business moving . The aim is to increase working capital to speed up the business of customers. The conditions of access are, to form groups of 3 to 5 members, with experience in the activity, who live in the same area of residence. The minimum amount conceived is Kz 100,000 (one hundred thousand kwanzas). The credit is paid in 12 (twelve) months.

✓ Kixinegócio: an individual credit, destined to make viable the business of the great customers. The goal is to increase the working capital to speed up the business of customers. The conditions of access are, to live for more than 1 (one) year, in the current residence and have an established economic activity. The minimum designed value is Kz 500,000 (five hundred thousand kwanzas). The payment of the credit is made in 12 (twelve) months.

✓ Kixicasa: a credit designed to support people with a small economic activity and low-income wage earners. The conditions of access are, to be between the ages of 18 and 60 and to be a resident national or foreign citizen. The designed amount is Kz 100,000/200,000 (one hundred/two thousand kwanzas). The credit is paid in 36 (thirty six) months.

Banco Sol is a financial bank thatsupports entrepreneurship and development programmes with public and privateinstitutions. Its interest rates are not informed in the products, theinstallment payments are fixed, the bank asks for guarantees. Its products are:

✓ Group Micro-credit is aimed at groups of 4 to 7 people, it is aimed at the creation of small family businesses - for small/medium farmers and for micro-enterprises. Working and fixed capital is variable, ranging from Usd 100.00 to Usd 2,500, with a payment term of 3 to 12 months, at the Bank's discretion. Microcredit is paid in fixed instalments, weekly, fortnightly or monthly, according to the group's business or the income received from that business. Group micro-credit is divided into two specific areas of activity - Commercial and Rural.

✓ Commercial Micro-credit: this is aimed at micro-entrepreneurs who need minimum values for the development of their micro-enterprise with a small structure in terms of organisation and volume of business, in a given commercial activity. The amounts granted to microenterprises range from Usd 500.00 to Usd 10,000.00, to be granted within an agreed period, ranging from 3 months to 12 months, with fixed instalments according to the client's business, which may be monthly, fortnightly or weekly, depending on the amount of income received from the business.

    ✓   Rural Micro-credit: it is intended for rural activities such as agriculture, fishing, etc. In agricultural credit, groups have access to the means necessary to develop their activities, namely inputs and equipment. The borrower is a group of four (4) to seven (7) people, with an elected leader. For agricultural micro-credit, the repayment period is 6 (six) months for the purchase of inputs and 18 (eighteen) months for equipment. The capital lent is Usd 5,000.00 and may reach Usd 10,000.00 in some cases for the purchase of equipment, depending on the needs for the development of agricultural activity.

BAI Microfinance is a financial banking institution that applies the funds raised in order to move the local economy and create new job and income opportunities. Its products arefocused on entrepreneurship and development:

    ✓   Young Entrepreneur: this is a credit for promoting self-employment and supporting young people with entrepreneurial ideas and no resources to start their activities in various sectors of the economy. It grants an amount of up to AKZ 1,500,000.00, with a repayment period of up to 24 months. Conditions of access: be between the ages of 18 and 35; have an account with the BMF, with a history of at least 3 months; work or live near a branch or BMF Bank Correspondent; no history of bad payment in the market; declaration of the market or walking card; cash flow (inflows and outflows); investment plan / business plan. And the guarantees are, deposit, attachment, blank booklet and goods to be acquired (if applicable).

    ✓   Micro Fixe: is a micro-credit product aimed at individual entrepreneurs (formal or informal) and micro-enterprises. Itgrants an amount of up to AKZ 7,000,000.00, with a repayment period of up to 24 months. Conditions of access: be at least 20 years old; income domiciliation; have a business in operation for more than 1 year; have an account with the BMF, with a history of at least 3 months; work or live close to a branch or BMF Bank Correspondent; no history of bad payment in the market; declaration of the market or walking card; cash flow (inflows and outflows); investment plan / business plan. And the guarantees are, deposit, attachment, blank booklet and goods to be acquired (if applicable).

Kixicrédito is the only institution in Angola that meets the requirements specified by the concept of anecosystem of social enterprises, its socialservice with a hybrid model, empowers low-income families. Itis also the only one in the country thatreportsits activityto the MIX Market, the centre for financial inclusion, at the world level.

CHAPTER 6
SOCIAL MARKETING

Social Marketing is the study of the application of marketing in solutions to social issues. It appeared in the USA in 1971 by Kotler and Zaltman. From approaches of Business Ethics, Philanthropy and Corporate Social Responsibility (CSR). It evolved into Cause Marketing and Green Marketing. Social Marketing is a strategy for behavior change. It works as a tool, in favor of a necessary action to promote some form of change in social behavior, which makes the population aware so that they can change their habits. Its application does not annul businessmarketing , withcommercial character, because while it seeks to transmit an advantage of a product/service or brand, social marketing seeks to transmit the importance of actions related to the product/service or cause/brand. Initially it was practiced by government bodies and non-profit civil society organizations. However, within the scope of Social Entrepreneurship , these actions started to be used by Business Corporations , combining three distinct areas, which today are a trend of Social Entrepreneurship, (a) social needs, (b) social influencers and (c) technology.

6.1. SOCIAL MARKETING PLAN

The creators of the concept, Social Marketing, define it as a process of creation, implementation and control of programmes developed to influence the acceptability of social ideas involving considerations related to product planning, pricing, distribution and Marketing research (Almeida, 2004). Kotler and Zaltman thought of Social Marketing as planning for social change. For them, for an action to be considered social marketing it must meet the following requirements (Kotler & Zaltman, 1971):

a) Propagation of the purposes through the mass average, fulfilling the conditions of Lazarsfel and Merton;

b) Audience of social campaigns, meeting Wiebe's conditions.

McCarthy's 4 P's are defined in Social Marketing as (Kotler & Zaltman, 1971):

- ✓ Product is the creation of a service/goodnessfrom a social idea for a public/audience that thinks desirable and is willing to buy. This marketing requires more market research to design a suitable product/service than Business Marketing;
- ✓ Promotion is persuasivecommunication/campaignthrough strategies and tactics that will make the product/service acceptable and then desirable by the target audience;

✓ Point is the provision of an adequate and compatible distribution of the service/product through the service channels;

✓ Price is the representation of the purchase cost and the opportunity cost of sale. The opportunity cost measures the value proposition of the idea you want to deliver.

For Kotler and Roberto (1992) the result of the application of Social Marketing aims at inducing four social changes: (a) change in cognitive thinking; (b) change in action; (c) change in behaviour to improve personal well-being and (d) change in values.

The marketing plan isdefined as "a written document in which, in a systematic, structured and predictable way, through studies, the objectives to be achieved in a determined period of time are defined, as well as details of the programmes and means of action that are needed to achieve the objectives set out within the time frame" (Sanz de la Tajada,1974, apud Ancín,2018, p.71).

The marketing plan aims to clearly express the options chosen by the organization in the development of its marketing strategy in order to ensure its development in the medium and long term, translating the decisions originated from the analysis into actions (Lambin, 2000).

Many authors have created models for theelaboration of the marketing plan (Skacel,1992; Ambrósio e Siqueira, 2002; Westwood, 1991; Rocha, 2006; Kotler, 1998). The marketing plan, presented in figure 12, is a proposal to apply social marketing to marketing planning, in a simple and accessible way to any social solution, in order todescribethe marketing actionsfavourable to thesolution, theresults to be achieved, the conditions for the arrival and the conditions for evaluating the results. Describedin the following steps:

1. Analysis of social change

It allows thecomparison ofsocial evolution trends with the current position toenhance social development. At this stage of the plan, if you want to understand which development scenarios are most likely. The diagnosis is made on five levels: (1) existingproblems, (2) analysis of existingsolutions, (3) analysis ofpossible competition,(4) analysis of the distribution/delivery the solution and (5) analysis of favourable environmental factors.

2. Marketanalysis

It allows the development of a social idea that is viable and sustainable. At this stage of the plan, we want to identify the strategies to implement the social idea, through the *SWOT (Strenghts/ Weaknesses/ Opportunities/ Threats)* analysis, identifying the Strenghts - their own advantages applicable to their solution in relationto the capacity of other solutions; the Weaknesses - their own disadvantages influenced by their solution in relation to the capacity of other solutions ; Opportunities - environmental conditions (society, market, financial context, economic context, legal context, political context, institutional context) favourable to the development of the solution; and Threats - environmental conditions (society, market, financial context, economic context, legal context, political context, institutional context) unfavourable to the development of the solution   ; The strengths and weaknesses are then confronted with the opportunities and threats for the development of strategies to implement social entrepreneurship.

3. Definition of Social MarketingObjectives

At this stage it isofprimary importance to establish objectives to guide strategy selection. Marketing objectives must be appropriate to the value proposition of the solution. For Kotler and Armstrong (2007), the main marketing objectives are: (a) attract new customers by promising them superior values,(b) maintain and cultivate current customers by providing them with satisfaction.

The *DREAM* or *SMART*technique can be used to formulate the objectives .

- ✓ DREAM:
    - o Dated/temporary;
    - o Realizable / attainable;
    - o Exact/specific;
    - o Ambitious/ambitious;
    - o Measurable/ measurable.
- ✓ SMART (HEFLO):
    - o Specific/specific;
    - o Measurable/ measurable;
    - o Achievable/ attainable;
    - o Relevant/relevant;
    - o Time-Oriented/temporary.

The deadline for the objectives can be set at

- ✓ Long term: 5-12 years or more;
- ✓ Medium term: 3-5 years;
- ✓ Short term: 1- 3 years;

One goal can be: (a) Quantitative and or (b) Qualitative.

4. Definition of SocialMarketing Strategy

At this stage it is intended to define the generalprinciples for the application of social marketing actions. Innovation and sustainability must be incorporated into these principles if the initiative is to be innovative and sustainable .The capacity for self-sustainabilityis guaranteed by the formulation of strategies that capture long-term value with the development of actions.Innovation will be characterized by the formulation of creative strategies that will guarantee the efficiency and effectiveness of results, while the growth objectives and the social business model must also be incorporated into social marketing strategies. The strategy will be defined through the formulation of actions. It is possible to use tools, techniques or models to guide the strategies.

5. Preparation of the Action Plan

The action plancorresponds to the transformation of the strategy into concrete actions by the implementation of the 4 P's. Establishing deadlines, costs and responsibilities, for an effective use of the marketing plan, is essential, because it quantifies all the planned actions, which allows the control of the plan's execution on a daily basis. The 5W2H technique is normally used to draw up the action plan.

6. Preparation of the Profit and Loss Statement

Models should be developed for the demonstration of results in panel structures or others thatmake it possible to visualise graphically, quantitatively and/or qualitatively the evolution of indicators. An evaluation system should be set up to define the tools for inputting data into the system, which are essential for reporting.

7. Preparation of the Evaluation of Results.

The evaluation and control of a Marketing Plan allows the difference between expected and actual performance to be reduced, guaranteeing its effectiveness. Therefore, the control must be done, during the actions and after, with the evaluation of the results. It is importantfor the control of the plan that periodic review meetings take place throughout the year. Strategies must be constantly discussed and adjusted to uncontrollable changes in the environment. Monitoring is done periodically (month or quarter), so the project can analyse the developmentof the objectives, visualise the positive and negative facts and make adjustments to the course when necessary. At least three types of monitoring can beapplied to evaluate the results:

✓ Strategic control is the verification of the fulfilment of marketing objectives, carried out by means of an instrument known as a marketing audit, which is a periodic (annual), comprehensive, systematic and independent review. The purpose of the audit is to determine the causes of the marketing plan implementation problem and to recommend a corrective action plan to improve the effectiveness of marketing actions;

✓ Control of the annual action plan is the daily administration of the marketing effort and results indicators in order to certify at what pace the objectives are being achieved. The analysis tools use the information from the reports created by the evaluation system;

✓ Efficiency control is the evaluation of the efficiency of the indicators selected to measure the marketing plan. It is done through technical or scientific studies.

Table 12: SocialMarketing Plan Structure

0	Executive Summary;
1	**Analysis of the needs for social change:**
	1. analysis of the problems,
	2.analysis of the solutions,
	3.analysis of competition,
	4. analysis ofdistribution and
	5.macro environment analysis.
2	**Market Analysis:**
	1. analysis of opportunities,
	2. analysis of meaças ,
	3. analysis of theforces and
	4. analysis ofweaknesses
3	**Definition of Social MarketingObjectives;**
4	**Definition of SocialMarketing Strategies;**
5	**Preparation of the Action Plan;**
6	**Preparation of the Profit and Loss Statement;**
7	**Preparation of the Evaluation of Results.**

Source: own elaboration

6.2 PREPARING THE *PITCH*

The Pitch is a clear and objective presentation of the main points of your business to *stakeholders* with the intention of arousing the interest of the viewer. Chart 13 below shows how the types of pitch's are distinguished.

Types of pitch's

1. *Tweet*: Up to 140 characters, it 's basically your business concept in one sentence. The ideal is to signal what you do and for whom. It is a sentence of approximately 3 seconds of speech, responsible for the first impression about your business. For example, *Youtube*, in the beginning, used a metaphor with another existing business model to facilitate the understanding of the service and positioned itself as "flickr of the videos"

.

2. *Lift*: Up to 1minute, the lift pitch (in literal translation) is important to perform at events, in networking moments, among others. But, what is important to focus on? Besidesthe tweet pitch, here we talka little more ,leaving a taste to the audience of "I want to know more about?

3. *5 minute pitch*: From 3 to 5 minutes you start to create more body and detail about your product/service. Besides the points mentioned in *Elevator Pitch* (problem, solution, business model and differential), hereyou can talk a little more about the market, theteam that composes the business. At the beginning of the *pitch,* to connect with the audience or "break the ice", a little *storytelling* helps a lot. If you have 5 minutes, you can also talk about the results and the competition. The financial part will depend a loton the type of audience. If you're *pitching* to an investor, that's a very important point. So always study the audience or interlocutor first, to find outwhat points you should focuson .

4. *10 minute pitch*: the opportunity stage ofa presentation of more than 7 minutes, usually takes place in a more focused meeting with an audience that has already had information about the initiative. Therefore, in this *pitch*, any information about the feasibility of the solution is important. The marketing and sales force, the team 's differential, theorganisational structure and activities can be presented.

Table 13: PITCH's characteristics

Weather	1 minute	3 to 5 minutes	7 to 10 minutes	10 to 20 minutes
Focus	objectivity	Deepening the data	Use support material	Involving the audience
Content	Value proposition	Simple social business plan	Social Business Plan with financial projections	*Storytelling*
Speech	Rhetoric	Contextualized technician	Rational	Emotional reflective

Source: own elaboration

An example ofpitch Elevator is Dazideia:

"Dazideia is a catalyst community for innovation that connects people and ideas. Its purpose is to boost the success of innovative businesses through events, content and connections with partner institutions".

This *pitch* features the followingmodel:

For [*target audience*] who are dissatisfied with [*problem*], our product is a [*product category or explanation*] that provides [*main differential or function*] different from [*current alternative*].

The structure of the Pitch can fulfil the following steps:

1. Develop the business model: use the "Canvas Model"structure to present critical factors of your business model;

Building the business idea: using the flow chart of the problem and solution tree and the definition of the value proposition to present the idea;

3. Fundraising: presenting a funding scenario. From the existing financing options, choose the one that best suitsthe purposes of the venture;

4. Choose the best organisationalstructure: present the legal and organisational structure of the enterprise;

5. Forming the working team: presenting the collaborating staff according to their competences and functions;

6. Define the activities: present the action plan of the activities necessary to realize the value proposal;

7. Measuring the social impact: presenting the structure (*framework*) of impact indicators.

Somestandards can be consideredfor a good pitch presentation. Below are some tips on how to prepare for presentation, how to get started and how to present.

How to prepare the pitch presentation:
- ✓ Be clear about your objective with the presentation:
  - o Making yourself known?
  - o Validate the new business?
  - o Find partners, customers, users or investor?
- ✓ Define what you expect from the audience:
  - o Please contact us?
  - o What test your product or service?
  - o To connect with your company through your website, newsletter or social network?
- ✓ Take ten deep breaths before you enter the stage, you will lower levels of anxiety and adrenaline and prevent forgetting.

Thinking about how to start a speech can always bring "the nerves to the surface". Here are some tips to start the presentation:
- ✓ Important market data: "Of every four children and adolescents, one has been treated in an offensive way on the internet, the so-called *cyberbullying*".

✓ Personal problem or struggle: "last week I went to 3 different places, losing almost 3 hours, to buy the products I use because of my allergies".

✓ Personal problem or struggle focused on the user: "Camila had to go to 3 different places to buy products that meet her allergy problem, until she met the company AllergiesXYX".

✓ Adesirable future: "imagine yourself, waking up every day quietly,having coffee with your children, gettinginto yourself-directed car andgetting to work without delays, with all the emails read, because you can read during the trip! Incredible, isn't it?"

Topresent the pitch:

✓ Speak slowly and rhythmically;

✓ Be enthusiastic;

✓ Be specific and concise;

✓ Look at the audience;

✓ Be declarative and do not use repetitions of verbal expressions;

✓ Use natural language and simple phrases;

✓ Do not underestimate yourself or exalt yourself, only differentiate yourself with your naturalness;

✓ Do not read, talk to your audience.

BIBLIOGRAPHY

Revised publications

1. Abu-Saifan, S. (2012). Social Entrepreneurship: Definition and Boundaries. Technology Innovation *Management Review*, February, 22-27.

2. Adams, R., Bessant, J., & Phelps, R. (2006). Innovation management measurement: A review. *International Journal of Management Reviews*, 8 (1), 21-47.

3. Almeida, P. P. (2004). *Social Marketing Plan: The Markthink Case*. Coimbra: Development Partnership "MARKTH!NK - investors in special people" Equal Community Initiative. ISBN 989-8034-01-7.

4. Alvord, S. H., Brown, L. D., & Letts, C. W. (2004). Social Entrepreneurship and Societal Transformation. *The Journal of Applied Behavioral Science, 40*(3), 260-282. doi:10.1177/0021886304266847

5. Ambrósio, V., & Siqueira, R. (2002). Step-by-step marketing plan: services. Rio de Janeiro: Reichmann & Affonso Ed.

6. Ancín, J. M. (2018). *The Marketing Plan in Practice* (22nd ed.). Madrid: Editorial ESIC.

7. Arvidson, M., Lyon, F., Mckay, S., & Moro, D. (2013). Valuing the Social? The Nature and Controversies of Measuring Social Return on Investment (SROI). *Voluntary Sector Review*. 4. 3-18. 10.1332/204080513X661554.

8. Ashoka (2001). Social Entrepreneurs, Sustainable Social Enterprises: how to develop business plans for social organisations. Editora Fundação Peirópolis. ISBN85663642

9. Bilali, H. E. (2018). Relation Between Innovation And Sustainability In The Agro-Food System. *Italian Journal of Food Science*, 30 (26). https://doi.org/10.14674/IJFS-1096.

10. Bishop M., & Green, M. (2008). *Philanthrocapitalism: How Giving Can Save the World*. New York: Bloomsbury Press, November, 298pp. Cloth. ISBN 978-1-59691-374-5

11. Bloom, P. N., & Skloot, E. (2010). *Social Scaling Impact: New Thinking*. New York: Palgrave Macmillan.

12. Dees, J.G. (2001). *The meaning of social entrepreneurship*. Center for the Advancement of Social Entrepreneurship at Duke Universityís Fuqua School of Business.

13. Dufays, F. (2019). Exploring the drivers of tensions in social innovation management in the context of social entrepreneurial teams. *Management Decision* 57(6): 1344-1361. DOI: 10.1108/MD-01-2017-0089.

14. Elkington & Hartigan. (2017). *Social Entrepreneurship Business Models: The Power of Unreasonable People*. Boston: Harvard Business Press.

15. Emerson, J. (2003). *The Blended Value Map: Tracking The Intersects And Opportunities Of Economic, Social And Environmental Value Creation*. California: Stanford University.

16. EVERIS (2015). *Social Impact Assessment Report*. Lisbon: NTT Data Comapany.

17. Ferreira, H., Cassiolato, M., & Gonzalez, R. (2009). *A Methodological Development Experience for Programme Evaluation: The Logical Model of the Second Time Programme*. Brasília: Institute for Applied Economic Research. ISSN 1415-4765

18. Filion, L.J. (1999) . Entrepreneurship: entrepreneurs and owners-managers of small businesses. *Revista de Administração da Universidade de São Paulo*, 34(2), 05-28.

19. FNQ (2012). *Performance indicators: Structuring the system of Organisational Indicators* (3rd ed.). São Paulo: National Quality Foundation.

20. Isenberg, D. (2011). The Entrepreneurship Ecosystem Stategy as s New Paradigm for Economic Policy. Em B. Global (Ed.). Obtido dehttp://www.innovationamerica.us/images/stories/2011/The-entrepreneurship-ecosystem-strategy-for-economic-growth-policy-20110620183915.pdf

21. Johnson, A. (2011). *Functions in Innovation System Approaches*. Chalmers university of technology. Department of industrial dynamics. https://www.researchgate.net/publication/253725869.
Yezersky, G. (2007). *General Theory of Innovation: An Overview*. Farmington Hills MI: Institute of Professional Innovators.

22. Kasparinskis, R., Ruskule, A., Vinogradovs, I., & Pecina, M. V. (2018). *The guidebook on "the introduction to the ecosystem service framework and its application in integrated planning"*. Riga: University of Latvia, Faculty of Geography and Earth Sciences Online ISBN number: 978-9934-556-39-5

23. Konrath, J. (2012). *Value Propositions Irresistible*. ©Jill Konrath. https://bacd.ca/wp-content/uploads/value-propositions-irresistible.pdf

24. Kotler, P. (1998). *Marketing Management: Analysis, Planning, Implementation and Control*. (5th ed.). São Paulo: Atlas.

25. Kotler, P. (1998). *Marketing Management: Analysis, Planning, Implementation and Control*. São Paulo: Prentice-Hall.

26. Kotler, P., & Armstrong, A. (2007). *Introduction to Marketing*. São Paulo: JC.

27. Kotler, P., & Roberto, E. (1992). *Social Marketing: Strategies to change public behaviour*. Rio de Janeiro: Ed. Campus, 1st ed.

28. Kotler, P., & Zaltman, G. (1971). Social Marketing: An approach to planned Social Change. *Journal of Marketing*, 35: 3-12.

29. Lambin, J.J. (2000). *Strategic Marketing* . Lisbon: McGraw Hill.

30. Marshall, R. S. (2011) Conceptualizing the International For-Profit Social Entrepreneur. *Journal of Business Ethics*, 98,183-198. DOI 10.1007/s10551-010-0545-7.

31. Moore, M. & Riddell, D. (2015). Scaling out, Scaling up, Scaling deep: Advancing systemic social innovation and the learning processes to support it. *Journal of Corporate Citizenship.* Doi: 10.9774/GLEAF.4700.2015.ju.00009.

32. Mulgan, G. (2008). Cultivating the other invisible hand of social entrepreneurship: Comparative advantage, public policy, and future research priorities. In A. Nicholls (Ed.), *Social entrepreneurship: new models of sustainable social change* (74-95). New York: Oxford University Press.

33. Mulgan, G. (2010). Social Innovation. In C. Azevedo, R. Franco, & J. Meneses (Eds.), *Non-profit Organisation Management (51-74)*, Lisbon: Economic Life .

34. Mytelka, L. K., & Smith, K. (2002). Policy learning and innovation theory: an interactive and co-evolving process. *Research Policy*, 31: 1467-1479.

35. Nicholls, A., & Huybrechts, B. (2011). *Social entrepreneurship: definitions, drivers and challenges.* Conferece paper.

36. OECD (1997). *Oslo Manual: Guidelines for Collection and Interpretation of Innovation Data.* Portugal: FINEP - Financier of Studies and Projects

37. Oliveira, E.M. (2004). Social entrepreneurship in Brazil: current configuration, perspectives and challenges. *Rev. FAE, Curitiba*, v.7, n.2, p9-18. Jul/dez.

38. Osterwalder, A., Pigneur, Y. , Bernarda, G., & Smith, A. (2014). Trad. Bruno Alexander. Value Proposition Design: *How to build innovative value proposals*. São Paulo: HSM of Brazil.

39. Peredo, A. M., & Meclean, M. (2006). Social Entrepreneurship: A Critical Review Of The Concept. *Journal of World Business, 41*.

40. Pinto, J. K., & Prescott, J. E. (1998). Variations in critical success factors over the stages in the project life cycle. *Journal of Management, Greenwich*, v. 14, n. 1, p. 5-18.

41. Rabechini, J. R., Carvalho, M. M. , & Laurindo, F. (2002). Critical factors for implementing project management: the case of a research organization. *Production, São Paulo*, v. 12, n. 2, p. 28-41.

42. Roche, C. (2000). *Impact Assessment of NGO work: learning to value change.* [edition adapted for Brazil ABONG ; translation; Tlscl Tradução c Interpretação Simultânea Escrita], São Paulo : Cortez : ABONG ; Oxford, England : Oxfam.

43. Salavou, H., & Manolopoulos, D. (2019). Pure and hybrid strategies in social enterprises: an empirical investigation. *EuroMed Journal of Business*, 1450-2194. DOI: 10.1108/EMJB-05-2019-0068

44. Sanson-Fisher, Robert W (2004). Diffusion of innovation theory for clinical change. *MJA*, 180: S55-S56.

45. Santos, F. M. (2009) *A positive theory of social entrepreneurship*. Social Innovation Centre. Fontainebleau: INSEAD.

46. Schumpeter, J. A. (1947). *The Creative Response in Economic History. The Journal of Economic History*. 2. ed. Cambridge University Press on behalf of the Economic History Association.

47. Skacel, R. K. (1992) .*Marketing Plan: How to Prepare It. What He Should Contain*. São Paulo: Nobel Prize.

48. Sucupira, G. (2015). Challenges of Entrepreneurship Social Business in Brazil. *Centre of Social Sciences of PUC*, Brazil.

49. Tcherneva, P. R. (2012). *Full Employment Through Social Entrepreneurship: The Nonprofit Model For Implementing A Job Guarantee*. Levy Economics Institute of Bard CollegeKotler, P., & Armstrong, G. (2004). *Princípios de Marketing*. 9. ed. São Paulo: Ed. Prentice-Hall.

50. Thompson, J. (2008). Social Enterprise and Social Entrepreneurship: Where have we reached? *Social Enterprise Journal, 4*, 149-161. doi:10.1108/17508610810902039.

51. Webb, J. W., Kistruck, G. M., Ireland, R. D., & Ketchen Jr., D. J. (2003). The Entrepreneurship Process in Base of the Pyramid Markets: The Case of Multinational Enterprise/Nongovernment Organization Alliances. *Entrepreneurship Theory and Practice*, 555-581.

52. Westwood, J. (1991). *The Marketing Plan*. São Paulo: Makron Books.

53. Yunus, M. et al. (2010) Building Social Business Models: Lessons from the Grameen Experience. *Long Range Planning* 43.

Unreviewed publications

1. Buvinich, M. R. (1999). *Tools for monitoring and evaluation of social programmes and projects*. Social Policy Notebooks, Discussion Paper Series, n.10.

2. ECLAC, (1997). *Formulation and Evaluation of Social Projects Manual of Social Development Division*. ECLAC: Joint Programme on Social Policies for Latin America.

3. Dazideia. Available at: https://dazideia.com/. Access on 30/08/2020.

4. Dib-Ferreira, D. R. (2011). The Assembly of a Project - Problem Tree / Objective Tree. ISSN 1678-0701, Number 34, Year IX. Dezembro/2010-Fevereiro/2011. Available at http://www.revistaea.org/artigo.php?idartigo=936. Access on 11/03/2020.

5. http://jornaldeangola.sapo.ao/economia/kixicredito_emprestou__500_milhoes_de_dolares. Access on 12/03/2020.

6. http://www.portosocial.com.br/2019/11/11/ecossistema-do-empreendedorismo-social-e-motivos-para-adota-lo-em-seu-negocio/. Access on 13/05/2020.

7. https://investigacionubv.wordpress.com/2012/03/17/metodo-altadir-de-planificacion-popular-mapp/. Access on 12/03/2020.

8. https://pmkb.com.br/artigos/o-uso-do-diagrama-de-arvore-em-projetos-problemas-solucoes-objetivos-e-estrategias/. Access on 12/03/2020.

9. https://sphweb.bumc.bu.edu/otlt/mph-modules/sb/behavioralchangetheories/behavioralchangetheories4.html. Acesso em 12/06/2020.

10. https://www.bancobmf.ao/creditos. Access on 19/08/2020.

11. https://www.bancosol.ao/Conteudos/Artigos/detalhe.aspx?idc=1641&idsc=1657&idl=1. Access on 19/08/2020.

12. https://www.dn.pt/lusa/angola-retira-licenca-a-19-instituicoes-de-microcredito-e-casas-de-cambio-9344347.html. Access on 19/08/2020.

13. https://www.themix.org/. Access on 19/08/2020.

14. IAPMEI (s/d): How to prepare a Business Plan: Your guide for a successful project. www.iapmei.pt (consulted on 27-02-2019). Access on 19/08/2020.

15. IPM. (s/d). Available at https://www.pmi.org/about/learn-about-pmi. Access on 27/02/2019

16. Kaleydos. Available at: http://kaleydos.com.br/mercado-de-impacto/ecossistema-de-impacto/. Access on 19/08/2020.

17. Lacerda, Botelho & Colussi. Planning in Basic Care. https://unasus2.moodle.ufsc.br/pluginfile.php/33879/mod_resource/content/1/un3/top2_1.html. Access on 19/08/2020.

18. LFA, Learning for Action Group. (2012). Evaluation Framework: A Primer. Disponivel em: http://sehub.stanford.edu/sites/default/files/Learning%20for%20Action%20Group%20Evaluation%20Framework%20Primer.pdf. Acesso em 23/08/2020.

19. Methodology 8D. _ Available at: https://engeteles.com.br/metodologia-8d/. Access on 19/08/2020.

20. Omunga https://www.omunga.org/index.php/sobre/. Access on 19/08/2020.

21. 5W2H Action Plan. Available at https://slideplayer.com.br/slide/5614817/. Access _on 13/06/2018.

22. Rocha, A. C. (2006). *The Strategic Business Vision and the Formulation of Competitive Strategies*: a roadmap for establishing strategic positioning and developing a marketing plan for micro and small enterprises. Instructional material used in the Marketing Strategies discipline. Florianópolis: Unpublished work.

23. Stanford University, Social Entrepreneurship Hub. Available at: http://sehub.stanford.edu/pro-roadmap. Access on 19/08/2020.

24. UDIA, (2018). Social Entrepreneurship Manual, NOVA SBE, Lisbon.

More
Books!

OMNIScriptum

Printed by Books on Demand GmbH, Norderstedt / Germany